◆◆◆

This book is dedicated to David,

who gave me the confidence to make it

a reality and to my daughters

Amy, Shirah and Anna, who gave

me many answers to my questions.

I am eternally grateful.

◆◆◆

Around the Family Table

365 Mealtime Conversations for Parents and Children

•••

Ronda Coleman

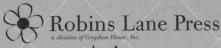

Robins Lane Press
a division of Gryphon House, Inc.

www.robinslane.com

Library of Congress Cataloging-in-Publication Data

Coleman, Ronda, 1957–
        Around the family table / Ronda Coleman.
               p.   cm.
    Includes index
    ISBN 158904-002-3
        1. Communication in the family—Miscellanea.
        2. Conversation.   3. Table-talk.   I. Title.
    HQ734.C5968   2001
    302.3'46—dc21   2001023724

Cover and interior design by Bartko Design
Published by Robins Lane Press
A division of Gryphon House
10726 Tucker St., Beltsville, MD 20705 U.S.A.
Copyright © 2001 by Ronda Coleman
International Standard Book Number: 158904-002-3

Introduction

As the mother of seven children, I know the importance of setting aside regular time to connect with our loved ones. One of the easiest places to do this is around the family dining table. Dinnertime discussions are a way for families and friends to join together and share their day's events, discuss values and learn more about each other. Dining together as regularly as possible is one of the single most important things a family can do.

Once around the table, it is not always easy to get everyone involved in meaningful, thought-provoking discussions. This book was written to change that. There are 365 discussion starters, questions to ask that will get everyone thinking and talking. They cover a wide range of topics—there are questions that cause you to examine your values, questions that challenge your brain or recall past events, questions that ask families what really matters to them—all the while strengthening a sense of togetherness and building fond memories.

The questions are written so just about any age group can participate. Families can involve very young children by modifying the question to their age level. And most importantly: none of these questions have wrong answers. It is important to be respectful of the opinions and ideas of others and to approach each discussion with an open mind and a listening heart. With that simple rule in mind, you will enjoy many hours of great conversation and with those you love.

Enjoy.

around the Family Table

The Questions

1. Many people make resolutions to change certain aspects of their lives or personalities, but few resolutions are kept. Why do you believe it is difficult to make changes? What are the most difficult changes you have tried to make?

◆◆◆

2. If you are a child, you have been given the opportunity to change places with an adult for one week. If you are an adult, you may change places with a child for one week. What do you believe would be the best part of the change? What would be the worst?

◆◆◆

3. You have just finished taking a long, important exam. During the test, three students were caught cheating. The teachers fear more cheating may have occurred amongst the students. They decide to have the entire class take a re-formatted test. Do you believe this is fair? If you were the teacher, what would you do?

◆◆◆

4. Some people decide upon their death to donate some or all of their organs to a person who could benefit from the transplant. How do you feel about this practice? Is this something you want to do?

◆◆◆

5. Life is full of memories. What is the earliest memory you have? Was it good or bad?

◆◆◆

6. A common belief is that our bodies contain souls. Do you share this belief? Why? Can a soul be photographed?

◆◆◆

7. Hope is something that gives many people strength in the face of difficult situations. Describe a time when hope has provided you the courage to continue.

◆◆◆

8. People who have been blind from birth, who have never had the chance to see, are able to formulate pictures in their mind. How is this possible?

◆◆◆

9. There is a wildfire raging out of control a few miles from your house. The fire department is evacuating the area. The fire marshal knocks at your door and states you have ten minutes to get out of the house. What do you take with you?

◆◆◆

10. You have a teacher or a boss that you believe is unfairly treating you. How do you handle the situation?

◆◆◆

11. Many people believe in the existence of angels. Do you believe you have a personal angel? Have you ever had the experience of an angel helping you through a difficult time?

◆◆◆

12. You have been diagnosed with a terminal illness. You have a month to live. You only have one hundred dollars. How do you spend your last month alive? If you had ten thousand dollars, would your answer change?

◆◆◆

13. Fifty-one percent of the population of the United States is female. Why, then, are women in America referred to as a "minority"?

◆◆◆

14. Many of today's heroes are sports figures or Hollywood stars. If you were to choose a hero that was not an athlete or a star, whom would you choose? Do you think athletes and stars deserve the title of hero?

◆◆◆

15. Sometimes it is easier to tell the members of our families the things we do not like about them, instead of the things we do like. Tell someone at the table three things you like about him or her. Was this hard for you? Why?

◆◆◆

16. All of our life experiences, whether good or bad, help shape our personalities. Can you remember at least one experience that has had an impact on your life? How did it change you?

◆◆◆

17. If you were to give a speech to the whole country, what would you say?

◆◆◆

18. You are in the woods with three of your friends. The only way home is to cross a deep river. It is too swift to swim. A small boat can take two people across the river, but once it reaches the other side, it may not return. How do you decide who crosses the river and who stays behind?

◆◆◆

19. It has been reported that the United States spends more money on military programs than it does on education. Do you agree or disagree with this policy? Why?

◆◆◆

20. It is sometimes easy to talk at length about ourselves. It is usually much harder to be brief. Describe yourself using only five adjectives. Does your family agree with your description?

◆◆◆

21. Why do you think it is important to give and receive hugs? How does it make you feel when you receive a hug? How does it make you feel when you give a hug?

•••

22. Are you a Cadillac

or a Volkswagen? Why?

What kind of repairs

do you need?

•••

◆◆◆

23. Your best friend has gone blind and needs an eye transplant. If you donate one of your eyes, it would mean your friend's vision would be restored. Your donated eye would be replaced with a glass eye. Would you give up your eye?

◆◆◆

24. We have many holidays throughout the year to celebrate. We celebrate in many different ways and for different reasons. If you could create a new holiday, when would it be? Why and how would you celebrate?

◆◆◆

25. You are preparing to graduate from high school. A wealthy tycoon has offered you the following choices: A full scholarship to a top university, plus living expenses, or one hundred thousand dollars to start your own business. Which one would you choose? Why?

◆◆◆

26. Body piercing and tattoos have become very popular in the last several years. Many states have passed laws that prevent a person from having either until he or she is eighteen years of age. Do you think this is a fair law?

◆◆◆

27. Many world philosophies discourage owning many possessions. Are you the kind of person who keeps everything? What is so good about not having many posessions?

◆◆◆

28. Unfortunately, many of us are not satisfied with certain aspects of our physical selves. If you could change one thing about your physical appearance, what would it be? How do you believe your life would change?

◆◆◆

29. Seneca said, "Let tears flow of their own accord; their flowing is not inconsistent with inward peace and harmony." Do you believe our society supports this sentiment? Is it different for men and women?

◆◆◆

30. What are five of the best things that have happened in your life thus far?

◆◆◆

31. You have a choice: To kill a dog or a worm. Does one animal have more right to live than the other? Why?

◆◆◆

32. Do you believe you know as much about Latino, Asian American and African American history as you do about white European history? Why?

◆◆◆

33. If you could meet one musician from any time in history, who would it be? Why? What would you ask him or her?

◆◆◆

34. Vacations are great. You have to plan a two-week vacation with your family. You have ten thousand dollars to spend. Where do you take your family and what activities do you plan?

◆◆◆

35. Many actors and actresses are children. They spend much of their time on movie sets and do not attend regular school. What do you think would be the best part of being a child star? What would be the worst part?

◆◆◆

36. Some cultures believe that dreams are prophetic—they can tell the future. What is the best dream you have ever experienced? Did it come true?

◆◆◆

37. The Internet has opened new worlds for many people. It has also raised new concerns about the safety of children. What do you think is the biggest danger to kids using the Internet? How do you feel it should be monitored?

◆◆◆

38. You are in the grocery store and you notice a mother slapping a toddler across the face. The child is screaming. What do you do?

◆◆◆

39. You have been named "author of the day" and have been guaranteed a publishing contract. The one stipulation is that you must write a book about your life. What is your book's title?

◆◆◆

40. Emily Dickinson said,
"We turn not older with years,
but newer every day." In what ways do you
feel "newer" than you did a year ago? In
what ways do you feel older?

◆◆◆

◆◆◆

41. Many of yesterday and today's wars are based in religious conflict. You are responsible for ending these wars and finding a peaceful resolution. How do you accomplish this goal?

◆◆◆

42. A large corporation gives you unlimited access to supplies and money to invent something that would improve the world we live in. What do you invent? What do you call your invention?

◆◆◆

43. Someone offers you five million dollars to kill a notorious drug dealer, and guarantees that you will not be caught. Do you kill the drug dealer?

◆◆◆

44. Are you an oak tree or a weeping willow?
What are the differences?

◆◆◆

45. Honoring those we love is very important. Think
of the person that you love the most in your life.
Describe your feelings when you think of this person.
Who is it?

◆◆◆

46. You have just won a million dollars. The contest
rules state that you must dispose of all of the money
within a month. How do you spend the money? Do
you give any away?

◆◆◆

47. Statistics in the United States continue to show that women make less than their male counterparts for doing the same work. Why do you believe this happens? Is it fair?

◆◆◆

48. Family traditions are passed on from one generation to another. If you were to create a new family tradition that would be passed on for generations, what would it be?

◆◆◆

49. You have been selected to be a part of a scientific experiment. You have two choices: You may redesign your body to make it look however you choose, or you may redesign your brain to be five times smarter than you are now. Which do you choose?

◆◆◆

50. There is considerable controversy in America regarding tax dollars being spent on the space program. Some people believe we should spend money solving problems on Earth before we explore space. What is your opinion?

◆◆◆

51. What is the most important lesson you have learned from someone older than you?

◆◆◆

52. If you were in charge of the country for one day, what one new law would you pass?

◆◆◆

53. If you could change into any animal, what animal would you choose to be?

◆◆◆

54. You catch your big brother stealing five dollars from an adult. He threatens to beat you up if you tell. What do you do?

◆◆◆

55. What is the most effective way parents can teach their values to their children? What was the first value you remember learning?

◆◆◆

56. You are elected superintendent of your schools. Your schools have the required core classes, such as math, english, science, and history. If you were to add one more core class to the curriculum, what subject would you choose? Why?

◆◆◆

57. We have all had extremely embarrassing things happen to us throughout our lives. What is the most embarrassing moment you ever experienced?

◆◆◆

58. Friendship is an important part of life. We need to form bonds with people outside our families to help guide us through life. Why do you believe you are a good friend?

◆◆◆

59. Capital punishment—the practice of executing a person for a crime he or she committed—exists in many states. Some people speculate that not all of the people who have been put to death have been guilty. If you were on a jury, how could you be sure that the accused was guilty? If you were sure the accused was guilty, could you recommend the death penalty?

♦♦♦

60. Mistakes are a common part of life. There is not a human alive who has not made a mistake. What is the one mistake from which you believe you have learned the most? What is the one mistake you most regret?

♦♦♦

◆◆◆

61. If you could meet one famous woman from history, who would you choose to meet? What would you ask her?

◆◆◆

62. You are dying from cancer. There are no treatments left to help you. At the most, you have a month to live. You are very ill and riddled with pain. Would you end your life or wait to die naturally? Do you believe you should have the right to end your life?

◆◆◆

63. Your best friend works in a clothing store. He steals three shirts and tries to give you one. You know they are stolen. Do you take the shirt? Do you tell anyone?

◆◆◆

64. Every six minutes, a species disappears from the Earth through extinction. You are in charge of the Environmental Protection Agency. What is the first thing you propose to reverse this trend? What timelines do you Impose?

◆◆◆

65. You are given the choice between being a doctor or a lawyer. Both will pay the same amount of money. Which do you choose? Why?

◆◆◆

66. Many people believe the Confederate flag represents racial separatism and is a celebration of slavery. Others believe it merely signifies a part of American history. This flag continues to fly over some government institutions in the Southern United States. Do you believe this is right?

◆◆◆

67. Animal rights activists believe it is shameful to raise minks and other animals solely for the purpose of using their fur to make coats. Would you wear a fur coat?

◆◆◆

68. Do you believe there are any differences in the capabilities of men and women?

◆◆◆

69. You are writing an advice column for a local paper. You receive a letter from a thirteen-year-old who says she is running away from home. She thinks it looks cool and exciting to live on the streets with no one to tell her what to do. What advice do you give her?

◆◆◆

70. There are people who are atheists. They do not believe in the existence of a "God" or religion. Do you believe in God? Do you believe It Is possible to live a moral life if you are an atheist?

◆◆◆

71. Which is more important, the flower or the seed?

◆◆◆

72. Some lawmakers have considered raising the legal driving age to eighteen. At what age do you think people should be allowed to drive?

◆◆◆

73. Many say that those challenges which do not hurt us will make us stronger. What is the toughest challenge you have faced? Did it hurt you or make you stronger?

◆◆◆

74. Do you believe other life exists in space? Why?

◆◆◆

75. There are many debates about the right of free speech. Different groups frequently ask for bans on certain music, movies or books. Are there some things people should not be allowed to say?

◆◆◆

76. Are you an ocean or a river?

◆◆◆

77. A famous basketball player displayed questionable behavior during a game. He was criticized because there were so many children watching. When approached, he stated, "I am no one's role model." Do you believe sports figures should behave as responsible role models?

◆◆◆

78. Life is full of conflicts. We have disagreements with family, friends, co-workers and classmates. What is the most recent conflict you have experienced? How did you solve it?

◆◆◆

79. Due to continued advancements in health care, people are living longer lives. Describe what you will be like when you are ninety.

◆◆◆

80. You have won ten thousand dollars in an interior design contest. Decorate your room however you choose. Describe what your room would look like.

‹‹‹

81. Newness and growth can come to every family with the changing seasons or a new exciting event, like the birth of a sibling or an accomplishment of a family member. Plan a celebration of something for you and your loved ones. What would your celebration consist of? What would it be for?

‹‹‹

◆◆◆

82. In this day of increased crime including theft, violence and vandalism, why do you think most people continue to return their library books?

◆◆◆

83. What scares you the most about growing old?

◆◆◆

84. You are a judge in a custody battle. Both parents love their children and take very good care of them. There is nothing adverse in either of their backgrounds. To whom do you award custody of the children?

◆◆◆

85. Who do you think was, or is, the greatest athlete of all time? What makes him or her great?

◆◆◆

86. You have been sent to live on an uninhabited island for one year. You may take five people with you. Name them.

◆◆◆

87. You have been in a tragic car accident. When you awaken, the doctor tells you he must remove one of your arms or one of your legs. Which do you choose to have removed?

◆◆◆

88. You face two paths. One is very short, steep, rocky, and dangerous to pass. The other is extremely long, flat, easy, and safe. Both paths end at the same point. Which do you choose to walk?

◆◆◆

89. Alice Walker said, "If art doesn't make us better, then what on Earth is it for?" Describe ways in which art can enrich your life.

◆◆◆

90. You have been given the responsibility to name this year's Person of the Year. Whom do you choose? Why?

◆◆◆

91. Do you believe parents automatically deserve respect from their children, or do you believe they must earn it? How do you earn respect?

◆◆◆

92. It is often easier to laugh at others than at ourselves. Name a time when it was difficult to laugh at yourself. Why was it difficult?

◆◆◆

93. We feel a range of emotions throughout a typical day. What is the hardest emotion for you to express?

◆◆◆

94. Although women's sports are beginning to get more recognition, male sports continue to attract larger audiences. Why do you believe this is?

◆◆◆

95. Many people believe that loyalty is an important part of friendship. If you had a friend who was involved in something illegal, would you remain loyal?

◆◆◆

96. Today is Plan-Your-Epitaph Day, when each person decides what they would like to have carved on their tombstone. What would your epitaph say? If you had to write your best friend's epitaph, what would it say?

◆◆◆

97. Pretend you just won a gold medal in the Olympics. How would you feel? Now pretend you just won a silver medal. Would you feel differently? How?

◆◆◆

98. You have been designated to give one hundred million dollars to a health care organization to help find a cure for a disease. What disease do you believe is the most important to eradicate?

◆◆◆

99. Sometimes we do not ask questions because we fear the response we may get. Turn to the person sitting next to you and ask him or her one question you have always been afraid to ask.

◆◆◆

100. Love songs are notorious for pronouncing all of the great feats people would go through for those they love: They would climb the highest mountain, swim the deepest oceans, walk the sizzling deserts. What is one thing you would not do for someone you love?

◆◆◆

101. Describe what you will look like ten years from now.

◆◆◆

102. A father and his son are involved in a serious car accident. The boy's father is killed and the boy is critically injured. As the boy arrives in the emergency room the surgeon proclaims, "I cannot operate on this boy—he is my son." How is this possible? Hint: the surgeon is not a stepfather or a priest.

103. You are given the opportunity to wear an unusual, wild new fashion into public for the first time. Would you wear the new fashion right away, or would you wait to see if it became popular?

◆◆◆

104. What is the worst nightmare you ever had? How old were you?

◆◆◆

105. You were placed on a citizens' committee to decide if a rare fish should be placed on the endangered species list. If the fish were listed as endangered, the construction of three major river dams in three states would be halted. Without these dams, electricity prices in those states will significantly increase. What do you decide?

◆◆◆

106. It has been said that there are only two things a person must do: die, and pay taxes. If you could choose a third thing that everyone would have to do, what would it be?

◆◆◆

107. There are two pictures in front of you: one is a roaring ocean, the other is a snow-capped mountain. Which image best depicts your personality?

◆◆◆

108. What is the single most independent thing you have ever done in your life? How did it feel?

◆◆◆

109. It has been said that every man has three characters: that which he exhibits, that which he has, and that which he thinks he has. Describe your three characters.

◆◆◆

110. If you are a child, what do you most want to be when you grow up? If you are an adult, what did you most want to be when you were a child?

◆◆◆

111. The government has selected you to join a task force to suggest ways to end school violence. What is your first suggestion?

◆◆◆

112. Who do you believe serves the greatest purpose man or woman? Does society support your answer?

◆◆◆

113. You are the CEO of a large industrial corporation. It is brought to your attention that your company is dumping Illegal pollutants into a nearby river. If the authorities find out, the company faces huge fines and you may lose your job. What do you do?

◆◆◆

114. Professional football players earn millions of dollars a year, while most schoolteachers make less than forty thousand. Which profession do you believe serves the greater purpose? Is the wage difference fair?

◆◆◆

115. There are many differing opinions regarding America's immigration policy. Do you believe America should continue to allow immigrants into the country? How should the government decide who we allow to come?

◆◆◆

116. Some people take major risks in life while others play it safe. What is the riskiest thing you have ever done or would like to do?

◆◆◆

117. You find a wallet with five hundred dollars and full identification inside. Do you call the owner, or keep the money? Would your answer change if the wallet only contained ten dollars?

◆◆◆

118. America is well known for its protests. Many people practice civil disobedience and are purposefully arrested to draw attention to their cause. Is there any issue you feel so strongly about that you would be willing to be arrested?

◆◆◆

119. You have two hundred billion dollars and all the material objects you desire. What do you do with your money?

◆◆◆

120. Are you a candle or a light bulb? Why?

◆◆◆

121. Some Native Americans believe that trees contain spirits. If this were proven true, would it be harder for you to cut down a tree? How would you allow for the development of communities if there were laws that prohibited the cutting of trees?

◆◆◆

122. You have just been granted the opportunity to trade places with a famous person for one week. Whom would you choose to be? What do you think you would learn from being him or her? What do you think he or she would learn from being you?

♦♦♦

123. There is overwhelming evidence and thousands of personal testimonials that prove the Holocaust happened. In light of this, there are people who dispute the existence of the Holocaust. Why do you think that is?

♦♦♦

◆◆◆

124. Security is something we all desire in life. What is something that makes you feel safe? Who is someone that makes you feel safe? Why?

◆◆◆

125. Some people believe in destiny. They believe that our lives are planned before we are born. Have you had an experience that felt like destiny?

◆◆◆

126. Who is the teacher from whom you have learned the most? What was it about the teacher that made learning meaningful?

◆◆◆

127. Name the five most important objects you own.

◆◆◆

128. Common sense is described as knowing what to do without having it taught to you. Name a time in your life when you ignored your common sense.

◆◆◆

129. There are thousands of different types of religions in this world. They all possess teachings of prophets that prove their religion is the correct one. How do you know who is right?

◆◆◆

130. Are you a dandelion or a rose? What are their differences and similarities?

◆◆◆

131. What do you think is the best part of being a police officer? What is the worst?

◆◆◆

132. When was the last time you laughed so hard your ribs hurt? What was so funny?

◆◆◆

133. You just received a gold record for a song you wrote about your family. What is the title of the song? Why do so many people like it?

◆◆◆

134. Name one person in your life in whom you have total trust. Name one person who you believe has total trust in you. How do you earn trust?

◆◆◆

135. In America, in the year 2000, hundreds of thousands of moms across the nation marched in protest demanding that the government impose stricter gun laws. Why do you think so many mothers would march for such a cause? What do you think the gun laws should be?

◆◆◆

136. People who have a lot of money and no time we call rich. People who have a lot of time and no money we call poor. Why is this? Is this true?

◆◆◆

137. Man's sense of curiosity has led him on many adventures and to many amazing discoveries. What is one thing you are very curious about and would like to explore?

◆◆◆

138. Health studies have proven that holding or petting a small dog or cat can reduce blood pressure and stress levels in humans. How do you feel when you hold an animal? What is your best memory of an animal?

◆◆◆

139. You are ordered into isolation for a month. You are allowed to take four books with you. Which four books are they?

◆◆◆

140. What are values? Where do they come from?

◆◆◆

141. You are appointed King or Queen of a wealthy country. What is one gift you would give to all the people of your kingdom?

◆◆◆

142. What is a family? Describe your idea of the perfect family.

◆◆◆

143. Many of us grow up with definite ideas of what we want to do In life. Sometimes our families have different plans for our lives. Do you believe it is more important to please your family or yourself? Has there ever be a time when you have done something to please someone else?

◆◆◆

144. You are stranded on an elevator. A voice comes over the loudspeaker and tells you that it will be two hours before the elevator will be fixed. There is a deaf man on the elevator with you. You do not know sign language and do not have a pen or paper. How do you manage to communicate this message to the deaf man?

◆◆◆

145. Untamed fear prevents us from moving forward. Some people believe that racism is based in fear. If this is true, how could you help someone overcome his or her fear of other races?

◆◆◆

146. What is waiting at the other end of your rainbow?

◆◆◆

147. There is no such thing as a "self-made" man. Everyone who has ever done a kind deed for us, or spoken a word or encouragement to us, has entered into the make-up of our thoughts, as well as our successes. Name five people who have had the most to do with helping you become who you are.

◆◆◆

◆◆◆

148. Why is it so hard to lose? How does it make you feel? Is losing as important as winning?

◆◆◆

149. There continue to be many people in the world who live with little or no electricity. Describe how your life would be different if you had no electricity. What would be the hardest electrical convenience to live without?

◆◆◆

150. Would you be willing to die for your country?

◆◆◆

151. Where does hate come from? When babies are born, do they know hate?

◆◆◆

152. What is the best thing about you? What is the worst thing?

◆◆◆

153. Drunk drivers kill many innocent people. If you were a judge, what sentence would you impose on a first-time offender? What sentence would you give a third-time offender?

◆◆◆

154. What has a larger purpose on Earth, the oceans or the deserts?

◆◆◆

155. Gossip can be very destructive to another person's character. Have you ever been negatively affected by gossip? Do you still gossip?

◆◆◆

156. Do parents owe children, or do children owe parents?

◆◆◆

157. If you had unlimited time and resources, what is the most important gift you would like to give to the Earth?

◆◆◆

158. You are camping with friends. In the camping area where you are staying there is a stack of firewood bundles. There is a lock box by the wood that says, "FIREWOOD—5 DOLLARS A BUNDLE." No one is around. Do you take a bundle and leave five dollars, or do you just take the wood?

◆◆◆

159. Admitting mistakes is a very hard thing for most people. What is the easiest way you know to admit you made a mistake?

◆◆◆

160. What is more valuable, emeralds or concrete?

◆◆◆

161. You have been given five million dollars. You may keep a million of them, but you must give one million each to four other people. Who are the four people you choose?

◆◆◆

162. There are some people in the world who believe it is funny to ridicule those who are different or disabled. List three possible reasons that someone might ridicule another person.

◆◆◆

163. Are you the sun or the moon?

◆◆◆

164. Life has a way of teaching us many lessons. What is the very first lesson you remember learning in your life?

◆◆◆

165. Should the American government pay restitution to the families of the country's former slaves?

◆◆◆

166. Do you think Americans should have the right to burn or otherwise desecrate the flag?

◆◆◆

167. In 1924, Native Americans were proclaimed American citizens. Does anything about that seem unusual?

◆◆◆

168. Where does love come from?

◆◆◆

169. If you could spend the day with any father in the world, whom would you choose? Why?

◆◆◆

170. Walt Disney once said, "It is kind of fun to do the impossible." What is something you think is impossible but you would like to do anyway?

◆◆◆

171. What is one change you would like to see in your family? What could you do to make this change a reality?

◆◆◆

172. President Lincoln is remembered for declaring that all slaves would be freed on January 1, 1863. If you were President today, what one thing would you like to be remembered for?

◆◆◆

173. Summer is a time of fun
and outdoor activities. You are a camp
leader. What activities will you plan for the
kids? What rules will you impose?

◆◆◆

◆◆◆

174. The government has just announced that effective immediately, three days out of each week television will not be allowed. How will this change the country?

◆◆◆

175. Pass on the best advice you know to the person sitting next to you.

◆◆◆

176. Some people have been pronounced legally dead only to be brought back to life. If this happened to you, in what ways would it change your life?

◆◆◆

177. The consumption of alcohol costs millions of dollars in health- and crime-related costs. Alcohol is legal, but drugs are illegal. Why?

◆◆◆

178. If you went blind today, what is the one thing you would miss seeing the most?

◆◆◆

179. Some health experts believe that the touch of one human to another can have healing properties. Can you name a time when someone's touch made you feel better? Why do you think this is?

◆◆◆

180. Which is harder: to be rich and become poor, or to be poor and become rich? Why?

◆◆◆

181. We all know that smoking cigarettes is harmful, but some people choose to smoke them anyway. Have you ever done something that you knew was a bad idea? Do you have regrets?

◆◆◆

182. Martin Luther King once said, "In the end, we will remember not the words of our enemies but the silence of our friends." Has there been a time when your friend was in trouble, but you didn't say anything?

◆◆◆

183. Many people like to collect certain items. What do you collect? What do you believe your collection says about your personality? If you do not collect anything, what does that say about you?

◆◆◆

184. Whether we know them or not, we all have grandparents. They can be a wealth of wisdom. If you can or could, what three questions would you like to ask them?

◆◆◆

185. A child is very ill and is waiting for a kidney transplant. The child's family has no insurance and has only raised one-half of the needed money. Another child is also ill and waiting for a kidney. This child's family has insurance that will cover the cost. Who should receive the kidney?

◆◆◆

186. Does a nation have to have a strong military to be powerful? Does a person have to be physically strong to be powerful?

◆◆◆

187. Imagine there is a Heaven and you are waiting to get in. You will be judged on whether or not you have accomplished your goals so far in life. How will you do?

◆◆◆

188. A popular 1960s song said, "What the world needs now is love." What do you think the world needs now?

◆◆◆

189. Mohandas Gandhi said, "The most heinous and the most cruel of crimes of which history has recorded have been committed under the cover of religion or equally as noble motives." If religion teaches us to be kind to one another, how could this be?

◆◆◆

190. Are you a star or a circle? Why?

◆◆◆

191. What is the best sound on Earth? When was the last time you heard it?

◆◆◆

192. You are the mayor of your city and you receive a large private donation of money. You may choose to spend the money to hire more police or to hire more teachers. Which do you choose to hire?

◆◆◆

193. If you could be anyone in the world, who would you be?

◆◆◆

194. What is the one single virtue that can make a person great?

◆◆◆

195. Name one stereotype you
used to believe was true but now know is
false. What changed your mind?

◆◆◆

◆◆◆

196. You are in a parking lot, and you notice a person pulling into a disabled parking spot even though they don't have a permit to park there. When they get out of their car, they are obviously not disabled in any way. What do you do?

◆◆◆

197. How do you think countries get their names? If you could rename your country, what name would you choose?

◆◆◆

198. John Lubbock said, "Earth and sky, woods and fields, lakes and rivers, the mountains and the sea are excellent schoolmasters and teach some of us more than we can learn from books." What is something you have learned from the Earth?

◆◆◆

199. Name three of the easiest ways someone can make you smile. Name three of the easiest ways you can make yourself smile.

◆◆◆

200. What is the best way to show someone you love him or her?

◆◆◆

201. What is more valuable: The life of a ten-year-old child or the life of a forty-year-old adult?

◆◆◆

202. For various reasons, you have decided that you must end one of your friendships. You do not want to hurt your friend's feelings. What do you do?

◆◆◆

203. What makes your family unique?

◆◆◆

204. Are all people created equal? Are all people treated equally?

◆◆◆

205. Do you remember the good things people say about you better than the bad, or vice versa? Why do you think that is?

◆◆◆

206. There is a saying that the best way to cheer yourself up is to cheer someone else up. Do you believe this works? Why?

◆◆◆

207. You have been chosen to redesign your country's flag. What will it look like?

◆◆◆

208. Many young women in the world are participating in dangerous diets. Do you think advertising aimed at young people contributes to this problem? If so, name some ads that you think might contribute to the problem.

◆◆◆

209. Some large corporations have their products produced in third world sweatshops in order to generate larger profits for themselves and their shareholders. If you knew this was the practice of a company, would you continue to buy their goods? Would you buy stock in the company?

◆◆◆

210. Imagine you just turned seventy years old. Your family and friends are throwing you a large birthday party. Look around and name the people that are at your party.

◆◆◆

211. Many parents are choosing to homeschool their children. What do you think are the advantages of homeschooling? What are its disadvantages?

◆◆◆

212. You have been chosen to pick a new National Anthem for your country. The stipulation is that it must be a song already written. What song do you choose?

◆◆◆

213. If you could turn time back to any memory in your life, what experience would you like to relive?

◆◆◆

214. Name three of the most desirable traits a person can have. Name three of the least desirable traits a person can have. How many of these traits do you have?

◆◆◆

215. Do you think there will be a need in the future to use nuclear weapons?

◆◆◆

216. Are you lightning or thunder? Which is more powerful?

◆◆◆

217. What is mercy? Should we always show it or are there times we should set it aside?

◆◆◆

218. Do you believe youth should ever be tried as adults when they have committed a crime?

◆◆◆

219. The day Harry Truman ordered the dropping of nuclear bombs on Hiroshima, Japan changed the world and war forever. Do you believe this was a necessary act, or were there alternatives that could have been used?

◆◆◆

220. Most of our music, movies, and television are rated according to the age for which the material is appropriate. Who should decide, and how should they decide, what is appropriate?

◆◆◆

◆◆◆

221. What is your favorite part of the day? Why?

◆◆◆

222. What is justice? Is it different for different people?

◆◆◆

223. Your teacher or boss has asked you to develop the five most important rules of the classroom or the workplace. List the rules.

◆◆◆

224. You have just won a full scholarship to any university of your choice. What do you choose to study? Where?

◆◆◆

225. Your best friend has asked you to falsify a document for him. You fear if you do not do this, it may jeopardize your friendship. What do you do?

◆◆◆

226. What is the most unrealistic thing you see in television families?

◆◆◆

227. François Chateaubriand once said, "There is nothing beautiful or sweet or great in life that is not mysterious." What is something you think is very mysterious in life?

◆◆◆

228. A recent poll showed that many members of Congress have been convicted of numerous crimes, including writing bad checks and abusing their spouses. Do you believe they should continue to hold office?

◆◆◆

229. A sheriff in a small town commented that he received more outraged phone calls regarding a news story about an abusive puppy-breeding farm than he had about a child abuse case that had aired on television a week earlier. Why do you think this is?

◆◆◆

230. In 1976, the first woman was admitted to the U.S. Naval Academy. Why do you think it took so long for women to be allowed into the Academy? Are women treated equally in the military? Should they be?

◆◆◆

231. If you could add a new member to your family, who would you choose to add?

◆◆◆

232. You are being sent to a remote island for two weeks. You are allowed to take ten items with you. What are they?

◆◆◆

233. What is the most effective way you know to present your beliefs to another person? Have you ever been successful in changing another person's beliefs?

◆◆◆

234. Is it possible to be completely honest at all times? Are some lies okay?

◆◆◆

235. Are you orange juice or Coca-Cola? Why?

◆◆◆

236. You have just won an advertising contest and you must create commercials that discourage kids from using illegal drugs. You are given an unlimited budget. Describe your commercials.

◆◆◆

237. Do you think it is harder for girls to be tall than for boys? Why is this? Where do these beliefs come from?

◆◆◆

238. We go through life changing and formulating new ideas based on our experiences and education. What is one thing you have changed your mind about?

◆◆◆

239. Why do you think women were not always allowed to vote? How would the world be different today if women were not allowed to vote?

◆◆◆

240. You have a time machine in your attic. You may go back in time to any period you choose, but once there, you must stay for a week. What time period do you explore?

◆◆◆

241. If you could bring one person back to life, someone you believe would have the most positive influence on the world today, whom would you choose?

◆◆◆

242. What is the hardest thing about being an infant? What is the hardest thing about being a teenager? What is the hardest thing about being an adult? What is the hardest thing about being elderly?

◆◆◆

243. Samuel Johnson said,

"He who waits to do a great deal of

good at once, will never do anything."

What are some very small ways you can

make a difference in the world?

◆◆◆

◆◆◆

244. Have you ever been lost? Describe what happened. How did you feel?

◆◆◆

245. If you could protect the population of whales forever by simply wearing a clown suit for the rest of your life, would you? What if you weren't allowed to explain to others why you were wearing the clown suit?

◆◆◆

246. What is more valuable, age or youth?

◆◆◆

247. What do you think are three great ways to honor those who are older than we are?

◆◆◆

248. Swimmer Mark Spitz was the first athlete to win seven Olympic gold medals. Is everyone capable of this type of accomplishment, or are some people just lucky?

◆◆◆

249. Do you think students should wear uniforms? What would this accomplish?

◆◆◆

250. You have a choice: You can vacation in a developed first world country, or in a remote third world country. Which do you choose? Why?

◆◆◆

251. Imagine it is the year 3000. Medical technology has become so advanced you are able to control how and when you will die. How would you want to die? At what age would you want to die?

◆◆◆

252. Some experts say the punishment should fit the crime. If you were a judge, how would you punish a convicted drug dealer?

◆◆◆

253. Name one person you admire and would like to be more like. Name one person who you believe admires you.

◆◆◆

254. Do you believe that male housepartners should share equal responsibilities with female housepartners? Do you think this kind of equality exists in most households?

◆◆◆

255. What has been the luckiest day of your life? What has been the unluckiest day?

◆◆◆

256. Are you a thinker or a doer?

◆◆◆

257. There is much controversy about the right to pray in American schools. Opponents argue that prayer in schools violates the Constitutional separation of church and state; however, the United States Congress begins each day with a prayer recited by the Congressional Chaplain. Does this also violate the law?

◆◆◆

258. What does prison accomplish? Are there any alternatives?

◆◆◆

259. What was the first time you remember being away from home overnight? Was it fun or scary?

◆◆◆

260. What would be the worst thing about being homeless? Are there any advantages?

◆◆◆

261. America is a country populated by immigrants and today many individuals are still coming to America in search of a better life. Upon arrival many seek citizenship. If it was up to you, how would you decide if someone should be given citizenship?

◆◆◆

262. You have just landed a multi-million-dollar contract to develop children's educational shows for television. Describe two shows you would develop. Who would star in them?

◆◆◆

263. Can you envision a society without money? How would it work?

◆◆◆

264. List the five most important traits a person can have.

◆◆◆

265. Is your soul chocolate cheesecake or angel food cake?

◆◆◆

266. Do you think the United States government wronged the Native Americans? Why or why not?

◆◆◆

267. What is the most important thing

a mother can give her child?

What is the most important thing a

father can give his child?

◆◆◆

◆◆◆

268. What do you believe is the single most destructive thing happening on this planet?

◆◆◆

269. You are walking down a city street and you notice a man attempting to steal a woman's purse. The woman is struggling. What do you do?

◆◆◆

270. What is the first toy you remember playing with? Do you still have it? If not, do you wish you did?

◆◆◆

271. Did you ever run away from home, or think about it? What was the outcome?

◆◆◆

272. What is the best way to discipline a child?

◆◆◆

273. What do you think is the biggest change the world will see in the next ten years? Will it be positive or negative?

◆◆◆

274. What do you think is the best way to teach responsibility?

◆◆◆

275. What is more valuable, snow or rain?

◆◆◆

276. What is the role of a student in school?

◆◆◆

277. In 1947, witnesses claimed they saw an object fall out of the sky near Roswell, New Mexico. The U.S. Army and Navy insisted it was a weather balloon, but the eyewitnesses stated it was an alien spacecraft. Do you think the Earth has been visited by other life forms? If we have, why would the government cover this up?

◆◆◆

278. Jesse Ventura, the governor of Minnesota, changed his mind about capital punishment after he took office. He stated that it was too much to be responsible for someone being put to death. How would you handle that responsibility?

◆◆◆

279. You are given a map to find a treasure. Inside the box is any treasure you want it to be. What would you endure to find the box? What is inside?

◆◆◆

280. Do you make your own choices or follow the lead of others?

◆◆◆

281. Are you a plastic picnic glass or a rare crystal goblet?

◆◆◆

282. What would be the worst part of being innocent and in prison? Do you think this happens often?

◆◆◆

283. Many people say Columbus discovered America. Others say that because America was already inhabited, Columbus did not discover it. Which do you believe?

◆◆◆

284. You agree to puppy-sit for a friend. You bring the puppy to your house. You leave for a few hours and when you return home the puppy has nearly destroyed your home. He has chewed up your socks, shoes and plants, and ruined your furniture and carpet. Do you hold your friend responsible for the puppy's actions?

◆◆◆

285. Is it ever safe to meet someone from the Internet? If so, when and how would it be safe?

◆◆◆

286. If you could give the children of this world one thing, what would it be?

◆◆◆

287. What is the most important country in the world?

◆◆◆

288. Should parents be held responsible for the crimes their children commit?

◆◆◆

289. What is anger? Where does it come from? What is one thing that makes you very angry?

◆◆◆

290. It is a terrible feeling to have your feelings hurt. It is also a terrible feeling to know you have hurt someone else. Which would you rather feel?

◆◆◆

291. What is truth? Who determines truth?

◆◆◆

292. If you could be any animal for a day, what would you be?

♦♦♦

293. You are moving far away and you only have one picture left in your camera. You want to take a picture that will remind you the most of your old home. What picture do you take?

♦♦♦

◆◆◆

294. The cloning of animals has sparked much controversy across the world. What do you believe are the dangers of cloning? What are the advantages?

◆◆◆

295. Are you more of a farmer or a stockbroker? Which is more important to the world?

◆◆◆

296. What is something you had in your childhood that no longer exists and you wish you had back?

◆◆◆

297. You have been ordered to give up your most prized possession. What do you give up? What does it feel like to be without it?

◆◆◆

298. Beauty contests seem to be very popular. Do you think babies should be entered into beauty contests?

◆◆◆

299. You are walking down the street and you hear someone yelling for help. As you get closer, you realize it is a notorious bully. Do you offer help or keep walking?

◆◆◆

300. Is there ever a situation or a person that is hopeless?

◆◆◆

301. You have an out-of-country visitor who has never been to your home. You have a large budget to spend. Where do you take your guest?

◆◆◆

302. You are in charge of a throwing a huge Halloween party. Describe what your party will be like. Who will you invite?

◆◆◆

303. Are you a secret keeper or a secret teller? Which is best?

◆◆◆

304. If you could become rich through illegal means, would you do it? To what extent would you go?

◆◆◆

305. What is more important to whom you are: your looks and hobbies, or your ideas and values? What is more influential in how people judge you? Why do you think this is? Is it the same for everyone?

◆◆◆

306. What do you do to find or create peace in your life?

◆◆◆

307. A genie appears to you and grants you three wishes. None of the wishes can have anything to do with money. What are your wishes?

◆◆◆

308. You have been elected mayor of Perfect Town, U.S.A. Describe your city.

◆◆◆

309. You have been offered a promotion at work, but you will need to relocate to another country. Your life would change dramatically. Do you take the promotion? How do you make the decision?

◆◆◆

310. Describe what the Earth will look like in fifty years.

◆◆◆

311. Little League baseball is a popular sport and taken very seriously by some parents. What is the worst example of sportsmanship you have ever seen? What is the best example you have seen?

◆◆◆

312. You have spent months researching and tracing your family tree, only to discover that one of your ancestors was a notoriously evil criminal. Do you keep this information to yourself or share it with others? Do you fear people would view you differently if they knew?

◆◆◆

313. You are guaranteed that if you try doing one new thing you will become expert at it. What would you try?

◆◆◆

314. What would you say to someone who was intoxicated and planning to drive? To what lengths, if any, would you go to prevent this person from driving?

◆◆◆

315. What is your favorite smell? Why?

◆◆◆

316. If you had to spend two years of your life in public service, who would you help? What would you do? Why?

♦♦♦

317. You come home and find your house has been robbed. What is the first thing you run to, hoping it was not stolen?

♦♦♦

◆◆◆

318. We have all heard the saying, "Life is not fair." What do you think is the most unfair thing about life?

◆◆◆

319. Do you believe that voting can make a difference?

◆◆◆

320. Would you rather have an empty castle or a full shack?

◆◆◆

321. Besides the physical differences, what are the major differences between males and females?

◆◆◆

322. You have written a five-chapter book about your life. What are the titles of the chapters?

◆◆◆

323. George Eliot said, "What do we live for, if not to make the world less difficult for each other?" What do you live for? What is your purpose?

◆◆◆

324. You are out hiking with your best friend. She falls down a steep embankment and is crying for help. If you try to reach her, you run the risk of falling also. What do you do?

◆◆◆

325. If you could have any supernatural power, what would you choose? How would you use your power?

◆◆◆

326. What are three things you would like to accomplish by the time you are fifty? If you are fifty or older, what three things would you like to accomplish before you die?

◆◆◆

327. You are a doctor and a dying man gives you a box of money. His last wish is for you to throw the money off of a rooftop and let it scatter. During his last breath, you promise to grant his wish. After he dies, his family members show up and tell you they are homeless and in need of housing. Do you give them the money or carry through with the dying man's wish?

◆◆◆

328. You have been given the opportunity to change the color of your skin. If you change you will be required to stay that color for the rest of your life. Do you change?

◆◆◆

329. In life, we all have things to be thankful for. What are you thankful for and what are five different ways you can say "thank you" to someone?

◆◆◆

330. You arrive at the first day of school and it is apparent that the classroom is overcrowded and the lessons are easily disrupted. What steps do you take to make sure you or your child gets the attention and education they deserve throughout the year?

◆◆◆

331. Is your house made of hay or bricks?

332. Buddha said, "A family is a place where minds come into contact with one another. If these minds love one another the home will be as beautiful as a flower garden. If these minds get out of harmony with one another it Is like a storm that plays havoc with the garden." How does your family handle problems or struggles so your garden is protected from storms?

333. If life is like a jigsaw puzzle, are you the lost piece or the last piece that fits?

◆◆◆

334. Do you think professional sports, such as football, are tampered with? Are some teams or players paid off to win or lose?

◆◆◆

335. You have fallen in love and wish to marry. You have the love and support of all but one parent. Do you still marry?

◆◆◆

336. What is the coldest you remember ever being in your life? Where were you? Who was with you?

♦♦♦

337. You have a friend who has different holiday traditions than your family. You would like to have this person visit for the holidays. How would you go about incorporating her traditions into your family's own? Would your family accept this?

♦♦♦

◆◆◆

338. Emma Goldman said, "I'd rather have roses on my table than diamonds on my neck." Which would you rather have?

◆◆◆

339. You have two hours to prepare a dinner for a famous celebrity guest of your choosing. Who would you choose, and what would you serve them?

◆◆◆

340. Are you a cloud watcher or a stargazer? Which one is more important?

◆◆◆

341. You are responsible for hiding a treasure. You can go anywhere in the world to hide it. Where would you hide it?

◆◆◆

342. You have a family member who is very ill and this will be the last holiday he will be alive. What kind of things would you do to make it special?

◆◆◆

343. Dorothy Parker said, "Four things I would have been better off without are love, curiosity, freckles and doubt." What are four things you would be better off without?

◆◆◆

344. What is the worst thing you have ever tasted?

◆◆◆

345. What do you believe is the worst possible breach of someone's human rights?

◆◆◆

346. What is your favorite holiday tradition?

◆◆◆

347. You have drawn a beautiful picture that you consider deeply personal. Someone discovers it and asks you to make it publicly available. Do you release it or keep it private?

◆◆◆

348. It has been said that guns don't kill people, people kill people. What do you think about this idea and how does it relate to the idea of gun control?

◆◆◆

349. For one year, you are allowed to trade houses with a friend. With whom do you trade?

◆◆◆

350. You are out sledding with some friends and one person is determined to slide down a very dangerous hill. The group is counting on you to talk this person out of taking this risk. What do you say?

◆◆◆

351. If ten million people in this country gave one dollar to charity, we could change the lives of many people. Why doesn't this happen?

◆◆◆

352. What are you the most proud of?

◆◆◆

353. You are flying home from college for a break. Your flight is cancelled due to bad weather and you are stuck at the airport. You are unable to make it home in time. How do you make the best of the situation?

◆◆◆

354. If you had to spend the holidays somewhere other than with your loved ones, where would you want to be?

◆◆◆

355. You have won a five-thousand-dollar shopping spree at a local mall. What would you buy?

◆◆◆

356. There are many different superstitions in the world. Some people believe in them and others do not. What superstitions, if any, do you believe in?

◆◆◆

357. You are taking a long car trip and you are only allowed to take one CD with you. Which one would you choose to listen to?

◆◆◆

358. We all worry, most of the time unnecessarily. What are three things you worry about that you wish you didn't? Can you remember a time when worrying changed anything?

◆◆◆

359. What is the warmest, safest, most pleasant memory you have?

◆◆◆

360. Do you like your name?

Does it fit you? If you could change it,

what would you choose?

◆◆◆

◆◆◆

361. What is your favorite lullaby? Do you remember anyone singing it to you?

◆◆◆

362. What is the most special gift you have ever received? What is the most special gift you have ever given?

◆◆◆

363. What is your fondest memory of the past year?

◆◆◆

364. Justice is frequently represented as a blind woman. How do you think this symbol represents justice?

◆◆◆

365. You have to give away one gift that you received this year to someone who did not receive any gifts. Would you pick your favorite or least favorite gift to give up?